Understanding
My Snake

Reptiles are becoming very popular pets and are overtaking cats and dogs as household members, however, their husbandry requirements are much more complex to keep them happy and healthy.

As a company who sees every day the shortfalls in caring for these specialised animals, we are pleased to endorse the series of "Reptiles are Cool" written by Siuna Reid, an experienced exotic veterinarian who cares enough to try and make a difference.

These books are very basic and provide simple steps and explanations of how and why we need to provide specialised environments for our pet reptiles to improve their captive quality of life as best we can.

—Pinmoore Animal Laboratory Services

REPTILES ARE COOL

Understanding My Snake

Siuna A Reid
BVMS Cert AVP (ZM) MRCVS

Edited by
Vivienne E Lodge

Copyright © 2014 by Siuna Ann Reid

The right of Siuna Ann Reid to be identified as the author of this work has been asserted by her in accordance with the Copyright, Designs and Patents Act 1988.

This edition published in 2014 by Siuna Ann Reid.

978-0-9576568-5-7

All rights reserved. Apart from any use permitted under UK copyright law, this publication may not be reproduced, stored or transmitted by any means, without prior permission of the copyright holder.

The guidelines in this book cannot guarantee a healthy snake. The author takes no responsibility for any subsequent illness or death.

Whilst every effort has been made to ensure that the information contained within this book is correct at the time of going to press, the author and publisher can take no responsibility for the errors or omissions contained within.

Printed in the Great Britain by Lightning Source UK
Book and Cover Design by www.wordzworth.com

CONTENTS

INTRODUCTION	1
SNAKES AS PETS	3
VISITING THE VET	5
THE HOUSE	6
SUBSTRATE & FURNITURE	7
HEAT AND LIGHT	8
ULTRA VIOLET LIGHT	10
WATER	11
FOOD	12
SKIN	13
EYES	21
DIGESTIVE SYSTEM	26
LUNGS	33
HEART	35
REPRODUCTIVE SYSTEM	38
KIDNEYS	42
NUTRITIONAL DISEASE	45
PARASITES	48
GROWTHS, TRAUMA & NEUROLOGICAL DISEASE	50
SKELETON	54
INDEX	56

Siuna A Reid

INTRODUCTION

I have been a vet for a long time and I have seen many changes in the kinds of animals that I treat. Over the past ten years there has been a huge increase in the number of reptiles that are kept as pets.

Reptiles are very different from mammals. The purpose of this book is to try to explain these differences and why they are important to the health and wellbeing of pet reptiles.

There are hundreds of different species of snakes being kept as pets. The onus is on the supervising adult to research the specific requirements before buying their pet. This book explains the importance of husbandry and some of the diseases that can occur if basic needs are not fulfilled.

Reptiles carry many different bacteria, one of which is salmonella. Although not harmful to them, the bacteria can cause illness in humans. Therefore, it is essential to wash your hands thoroughly after handling all reptiles.

There are many species of venomous snakes. These require a zoo license to keep and are not suitable as pets.

Later in the book you will come across the following symbols. Each one highlights a particular aspect of your reptile's care, relating directly to the health issue being discussed.

House

Furniture

Heat and Light

UV light

Water/Humidity

Food

2

SNAKES AS PETS

Buying a pet and looking after it is a huge responsibility. As a pet owner you have to make sure that your pet has somewhere suitable to live, has the correct food to eat and receives lots of care and attention. You have to notice when your pet is not feeling well and may need to be taken to the vet.

The most commonly kept pets are mammals such as dogs, cats, rabbits and hamsters. Humans are mammals too, so we generally find it quite easy to relate to other mammals and to realise when they are unwell or in distress. If you stand on your dog's paw he will yelp and you will know he is in pain. If your dog is too cold you will notice that he is shivering and if he is too hot you will notice that he is panting. If he doesn't eat his dinner you will realise that he is feeling unwell.

You have chosen to keep a snake as a pet. Snakes are reptiles and reptiles are very different from mammals. Your snake will not give you such obvious signals to let you know that he is feeling unwell, or too hot, or too cold, or in pain. His signs of distress are much more subtle and you will have to observe him very closely to make sure that he is healthy otherwise his suffering will go unnoticed. You should weigh your snake regularly as it may not be obvious just from looking at him that he is losing weight.

Many of the health problems which occur in snakes are related to some aspect of their environment or their diet. In this book we will first look at the correct housing and feeding for your snake. Then we will go through the body systems of your snake to find out how they work and what to look out for should things go wrong.

CAPTIVE BRED

Wherever possible buy a captive bred snake. Snakes bought from wild stock are often exposed to, and can carry a wide range of different parasites, bacteria and viruses. Buying a wild caught snake also encourages this unethical trade.

HOLIDAY CARE

Everybody needs a holiday! When choosing a suitable place for your snake to stay whilst you are away, ensure that he is not exposed to other snakes. If your snake is either living in isolation, or in an isolated group, suddenly placing him in an environment where there are other snakes could be dangerous. There is a huge risk of disease spread. Wherever possible, arrange for your snake to be cared for at your own home.

INSURANCE

Please note that snake health care is specialised and should they become ill treatment can be expensive. Insurance is one way to help towards the cost of veterinary care.

VISITING THE VET

At some point you may need to take your snake to the vet. This symbol, which you will come across throughout the book, indicates when you will need to seek extra help, medicine or maybe even surgery for your snake. Try to choose a vet who has a special interest in reptiles. Some vets take more exams so that they have extra qualifications for treating reptiles. If your local vets are not reptile enthusiasts they should be able to recommend a vet who is. If you have difficulty finding a suitable vet you could contact The Royal College of Veterinary Surgeons www.rcvs.org.uk.

THE HOUSE

Where will your snake live? You will need to buy a tank for him to use as his house. It is best to get the tank (and also the things that you put in it – see below) from a specialist reptile shop. Tanks made of glass or plastic are a good idea as these materials are easy to clean.

Within the tank you are trying to create a small world which mimics the kind of environment that your species of snake would live in if it were living in the wild. Desert species, like king snakes, need a dry environment. Tropical species, like the boa constrictor, thrive in more humid surroundings. Therefore it is very important that you fully research your chosen species so that you can create the correct living environment.

It is also important to think about where within your home you will place the snake's house. The best place is within a room that is used, like your bedroom or the main living room. Your snake needs to be somewhere with a constant temperature. Do not put his house beside a window or over a radiator as the temperature will rise and fall too much in these areas.

Snakes are escape artists so it is important to make sure that the roof of the house is secure.

SUBSTRATE & FURNITURE

Substrate is the material used to cover the floor of your snake's house. If you have a desert species you should provide him with sand. A tropical species needs a combination of soil and moss.

You will also need to put some furniture in his house. He needs to have somewhere to hide, especially if his house is in a busy room. You can buy him a plastic cave or you can use pieces of wood or log to make a hide. Plants such as vines can also be used for creating hiding areas. Natural plants look good but it is also possible to use plastic ones which have the added advantage of being easy to clean.

HEAT AND LIGHT

Life on Earth is supported by the sun. The sun provides heat and also light. Animals' need both heat and light to survive.

Mammals can control their own body temperature. The food they eat provides the body with energy and heat. If they are too cold they shiver and if they are too hot they sweat. These processes use up a lot of energy.

Your snake is a reptile and reptiles regulate their body temperature very differently from mammals. This is a major and vitally important difference. Reptiles are cold blooded (exothermic). This means that their bodies cannot produce heat from the food that they eat. Because of this they need much less energy from food to survive. A 100g reptile needs only 5% of the energy that a 100g mammal needs. To keep warm they need to bathe in the sun or sit on a warm rock. They have no hair, no sweat glands and do not shiver. This means that your snake will show no obvious signs that he is too hot or too cold.

You need to provide sources of heat for your snake within his house. This could be a heat bulb, a hot rock or an under floor heating mat. It is important that you know the temperature in your snake's house, both the hottest and the coolest areas. To do this you will need to use thermometers to check all around their house. A thermostat is a device that should be added to the house to control the temperature.

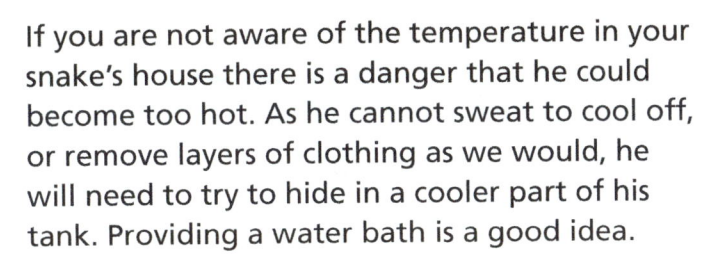

If you are not aware of the temperature in your snake's house there is a danger that he could become too hot. As he cannot sweat to cool off, or remove layers of clothing as we would, he will need to try to hide in a cooler part of his tank. Providing a water bath is a good idea.

It is more common, however, for a snake to find himself in an environment which is too cold. Cooler temperatures are unlikely to kill him, but will put a strain on his body and organs. His muscles, lungs, intestines and heart will struggle to work if they are too cold, and if this goes on for a long time it can lead to illness and even death.

ULTRA VIOLET LIGHT

As well as producing heat and light, the sun also produces ultraviolet (UV) light. This is a type of light which we cannot see but snakes can. It affects the skin and in humans it can cause sunburn.

Reptiles use UV light to make vitamin D3. This helps to keep their bones strong and healthy and enable their guts to absorb calcium from their food. To obtain vitamin D3 he will need exposure to UV light for 12 hours a day.

Snakes are not dependent on Vitamin D3 made by UV light. They are unusual because most of their food already contains enough vitamin D3 and calcium. However, snakes are exposed to UV light in the wild and it is still very important to provide a UV light.

Ultra violet light can be provided as a combination bulb or a UV tube. The tube needs to be no more than 30cm away from your snake. Remember that a UV tube will not provide him with any heat. The bulb should be changed once a year. Although the bulb may appear to be working, over time it will eventually stop producing UV light.

WATER

All snakes need water to drink. It is important that it is clean and regularly changed. Without water his body will become dehydrated. Dehydration can lead to constipation. If your snake becomes constipated he could die.

Humidity is also an important consideration when setting up your snake's house. When water evaporates it forms an invisible gas called water vapour. Humidity is a measure of the amount of water vapour that is present in the air.

In hot dry areas, like deserts, there is not a lot of water vapour in the air which means that deserts have low humidity. Rain forests are also hot but they have lots of water vapour in the air and so they have high humidity.

The level of humidity required for your snake will depend on what type of snake he is and therefore what type of environment he needs to live in. You can use a gadget called a hygrometer to measure the level of humidity in your snake's house to ensure that it is suitable for him.

Snakes also like to be able to immerse themselves totally. This can be done by providing a large tray full of water.

FOOD

Snakes eat live prey in the wild. However, it is illegal to feed live food to a snake in the United Kingdom. Most snakes eat rodents and day old chicks. Larger snakes will eat rabbits and guinea pigs. As your snake is kept in captivity you will have to buy food for him. This will usually be frozen and must be stored and prepared correctly to prevent your snake from becoming ill. Always ensure that any frozen food has thoroughly defrosted and warmed to room temperature before being fed to your snake.

Some snakes eat eggs, fish and frogs, and there are examples of snakes eating snakes!

The frequency with which you feed your snake will depend on his age and stage of development. When the snake is small, it is important to feed the correct size of food. Smaller snakes tend to eat more regularly. Larger snakes eat only once a week.

Many snakes in captivity do not eat for long periods. Although snakes are able to survive long periods without food, it can be dangerous for them if they start to lose a lot of weight.

Vitamin and mineral supplements are still needed. This can be provided by buying a multivitamin powder. These are sprinkled onto the prey prior to feeding to the snake. Fish eating snakes are particularly prone to vitamin deficiencies.

SKIN

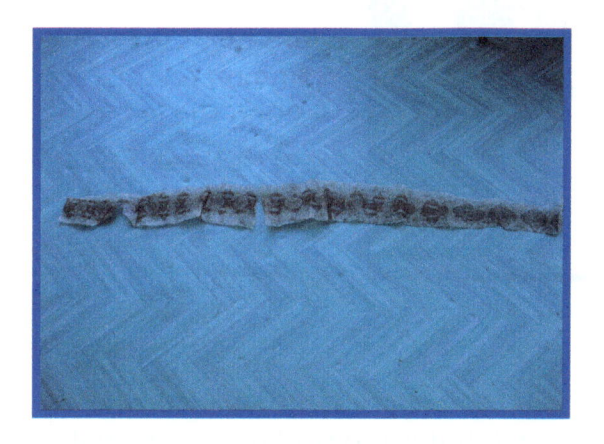

The skin is the largest organ of the body. Reptile skin is unique and has many functions which include protecting the body, providing camouflage and making vitamin D3.

SHEDDING (ECDYSIS)

When mammals grow, their skin stretches and grows too. Reptiles are different. Their skin does not stretch with growth. Therefore, the ability to shed skin is very important to your snake. When it is time to shed, your snake will produce a chemical which divides the old and the new skin. At this stage his skin will look dull and bluish. He will naturally rub himself against rough or moist furniture to remove his old skin. Snakes, unlike other reptiles shed their skin in one piece. You will now see his shiny and colourful new skin.

Snakes do not have proper eyelids. These fused and became see through thousands of years ago. When a snake sheds, he also sheds the top layer of his eye. This is called the spectacle.

It is important to keep a diary of how often your snake sheds.

DYSECDYSIS

Sometimes snakes have problems shedding. This is known as dysecdysis. It is one of the most common reasons for visiting the vet. Old skin can stick to the eye ball making it difficult for the snake to see.

Make sure that the temperature in your snake's house is correct. If it is too cold he will struggle to shed.

Lack of humidity is one of the most common reasons for failure to shed. You can increase the humidity by spraying the tank with water. Just make sure it is not too wet as this can lead to ulcers on the skin.

Any problems relating to shedding should be closely monitored and may require a visit to the vet.

SKIN PROBLEMS

ABSCESSES

Abscesses are lumps on the skin which are infected with bacteria or fungi. Damaged skin is a common cause of infection.

Check for sharp objects in the house.

Correct temperature will help your snake fight off infection

A good diet keeps the immune system healthy.

Make sure all furniture has smooth edges.

If your snake does develops an abscess he will need to have an operation to remove it. Fungal infections are very difficult to treat. A considerable amount of medicine may be needed to cure any disease.

BURNS

Thermal burns happen when snakes come into contact with an unprotected hot surface. This could be a heat lamp or a hot rock. Snakes seem to have difficulty detecting hot surfaces and do not react until serious damage has already been done to their skin.

Always check that any bulbs, heat pads or hot rocks in your snake's house are working properly to prevent burning. If the heat bulb is inside the house always ensure that it has a wire cage around it.

Minor burns may not need any treatment. However, serious burns will need veterinary care. This treatment may include creams and antibiotics.

16

TRAUMA

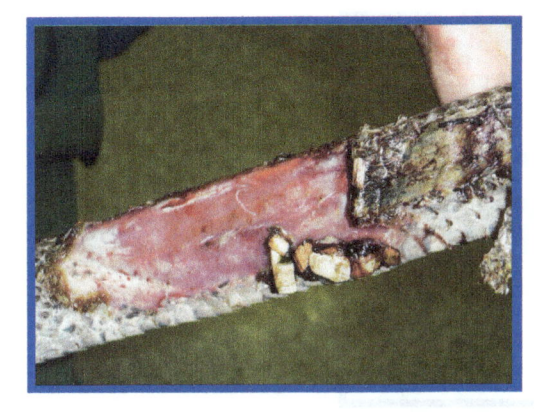

The skin can be damaged by sharp objects inside or outside the house.

Strimmer damage

Skin damage

Check the house for any sharp objects and remove them. If your snake is allowed to roam around your home, make sure he is supervised.

Check all the furniture for sharp edges.

Cuts will often need antibiotics or cream and in severe cases may require surgery.

MITES AND TICKS

Look for little black or red dots on the skin. The mites will breed in the reptile house. They bite the skin which causes it to become very itchy. Affected snakes are often restless and will rub their face and skin.

Ticks are more common in snakes that are caught in the wild.

The house will need to be cleaned thoroughly to get rid of all the mites and their eggs. Don't take your snake to a pet shop when you go on holiday. Mites can spread very easily.

The furniture will need to be cleaned and fresh substrate placed in the house.

The vet will be able to give you medicine to kill the mites.

18

RETAINED SPECTACLE

Snakes shed the surface of the eye when they shed their skin. If the spectacle is retained it can lead to blindness and difficulty when feeding.

Damage to eye from untreated retained spectacles

The house needs to be at the correct temperature to make sure that the snake can successfully shed his skin.

The correct humidity is vital to help the snake shed his skin.

Snakes like to rub against the furniture to remove the old skin.

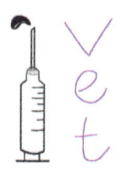

Retained spectacles have to be removed surgically by the vet.

19

BLISTER DISEASES (VESICULAR DERMATITIS)

Snake skin is sensitive to high humidity. The skin will blister and become infected.

The house needs to be at the correct temperature.

High humidity prevents the skin from drying out making them more prone to infection.

This condition needs medical attention. Antibiotics and veterinary treatment is vital.

OVERACTIVE THYROID (HYPERTHYROIDISM)

The thyroid gland is in the neck and is responsible for the amount of times the snake will shed. An over active thyroid makes the snake shed far more regularly than is normal for the age and size of snake.

This condition needs a visit to the vet.

EYES

Snakes have poor eyesight compared to other reptiles, although they still see colour and also ultra violet light.

Snake eyelids are quite different from ours. If you look at your own eye you will see that you have a big upper eyelid which comes down to cover your eye when you blink, and a much smaller lower eyelid. Snakes do not have eyelids.

The coloured circle in your eye is called the iris. This deterimines whether you have green, blue or brown eyes. The pupil is in the centre of the iris. Your pupil is black and round. It can become bigger or smaller depending the amount of light around you.

Snakes have round or slit pupils depending on whether they are a species that is awake during the day or night. Often the iris is the same colour as the pattern on their skin. The iris appear as slits when they are awake at night (nocturnal). Day time snakes tend to have a round pupil.

Snakes have tiny bones in the white part of their eyes called scleral ossicles. These help to give the eyeball extra strength.

EYE PROBLEMS

TRAUMA (DAMAGE)

Any trauma to your snake's eye could result in serious damage. This could happen in several ways. Examples would be, bedding caught in the eye or a scratch caused by a sharp object. An ulcer may form on the cornea. This is the transparent outer layer of the eye. Ulcers are very painful and in severe cases may cause the eye to burst.

To prevent eye trauma you should check your snake's house and furniture carefully for any sharp objects. Remember to take extra care when handling your snake outside of his house. Cage mates can also inflict serious damage if they fight.

If you suspect your snake has suffered any trauma to his eye take him to the vet immediately. Eye damage is an emergency and if not treated in time, your snake may lose his eye.

RETAINED SPECTACLE

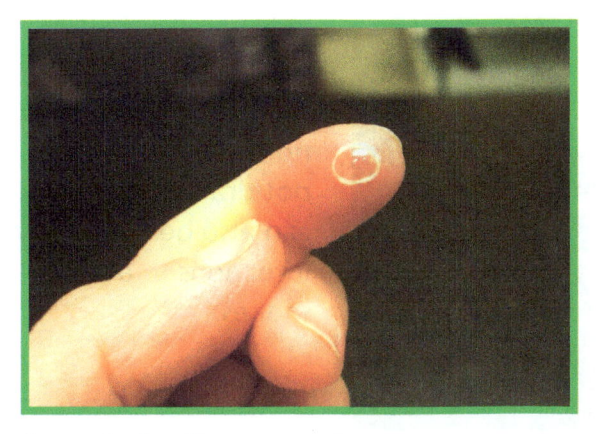

Snakes shed the surface of the eye when they shed their skin. If the spectacle is retained it can lead to blindness and difficulty when feeding.

A spectacle after removal

The house needs to be at the correct temperature to make sure that the snake can shed his skin.

Too humid and the skin will ulcerate and too dry makes it difficult for the skin to shed normally.

Snakes like to rub against the furniture to remove the skin.

Retained spectacles have to be removed surgically by the vet.

23

FLUID BEHIND THE SPECTACLE

This is a condition that is seen in young snakes, where the normal fluid does not drain away. It can also be caused by infections in adult snakes.

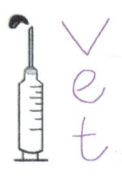

Vet: A visit to the vet is needed for this condition.

CATARACTS

As snakes age, the lens changes and becomes white. This stops the snake from seeing and may cause problems when feeding.

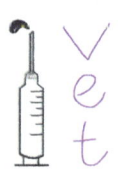

Vet: There is no specific treatment for cataracts. An operation to remove the cataract is possible in larger snakes.

MITES AND TICKS

Snakes do not have eyelids. Ticks and mites can live in the spectacle where they cause a lot of irritation.

Vet

Removal of insects from the spectacle can be difficult and is best done by a vet.

DIGESTIVE SYSTEM

The digestive system is the part of the body that converts food into energy. Left over waste is expelled through the vent.

The digestive tract of your snake consists of the mouth, stomach, intestines and vent. The vent is the reptile equivalent of the anus in mammals.

MOUTH

Snakes have lots of very small bones similar to teeth. When these break they regrow. In our mouths the roof is called the hard palate. The snake does not have a roof to his mouth. Instead he has a hole called the choana. Snakes have six rows of teeth. Two on the upper jaw and one on each lower jaw.

26

The tongue of the snake is forked.

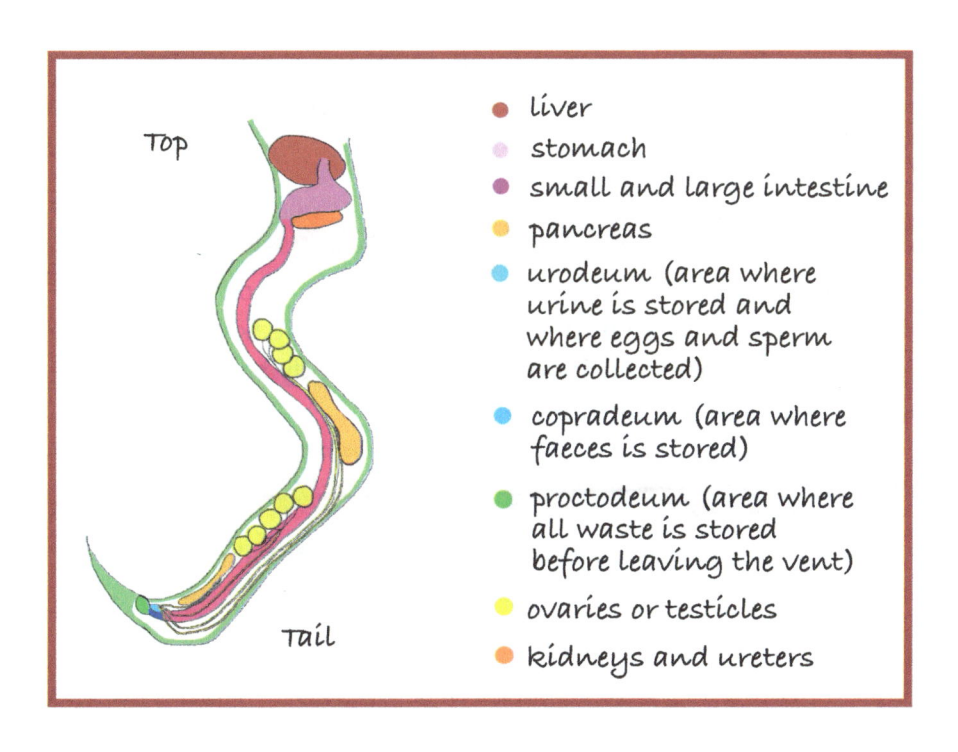

Top
Tail

- liver
- stomach
- small and large intestine
- pancreas
- urodeum (area where urine is stored and where eggs and sperm are collected)
- copradeum (area where faeces is stored)
- proctodeum (area where all waste is stored before leaving the vent)
- ovaries or testicles
- kidneys and ureters

STOMACH

A tube called the oesophagus leads from the mouth to the stomach.

INTESTINES

After the stomach the digestive tract continues as the small and large intestine.

VENT

The vent is made up of three areas. The food waste from the large intestine is stored in the coprodeum. The urodeum is the area which stores urine, and also any sperm or eggs (depending on whether your snake is male or female). Both the coprodeum and urodeum empty into the proctodeum, and from here all faeces and urine are passed out through the vent.

LIVER

The liver is the largest organ inside the body and has many functions. It plays an important part in the breakdown of proteins and fats from food. It helps the body to expel any poisons and other harmful substances.

PANCREAS

The pancreas produces juices which help to breakdown food.

PROBLEMS OF THE DIGESTIVE SYSTEM

STOMATITIS

Stomatitis is an inflammation of the mouth. It is commonly known as mouth rot. Stomatitis can be caused by viral or bacterial infection. It can also be caused as a result of damage to the mouth.

Pay particular attention to the condition of the house. Very active species such as corn snakes may need the glass of the house to be covered to prevent them from charging at the glass or plastic front.

Low temperatures in the house can lead to a weakening of the immune system.

Check the furniture in your snake's house to make sure that there are no sharp areas which could damage his mouth.

If you think your snake might have stomatitis have him checked by the vet.

29

FATTY LIVER DISEASE

Snakes need to eat regularly. Fatty liver disease is also known as hepatic lipidosis. Liver cells become swamped with fat, preventing the liver from working properly. It is very difficult to detect fatty liver disease. There are no obvious symptoms but a snake with this condition will stop eating. It is important to weigh your snake regularly to spot any severe weight loss.

Low temperature can cause loss of appetite.

If the food for your snake is too big it can put him off his food. Make sure you are feeding a good balanced diet for your particular species of snake.

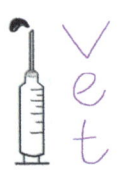

If your snake loses more than 10% of his bodyweight you should take him to the vet.

CONSTIPATION

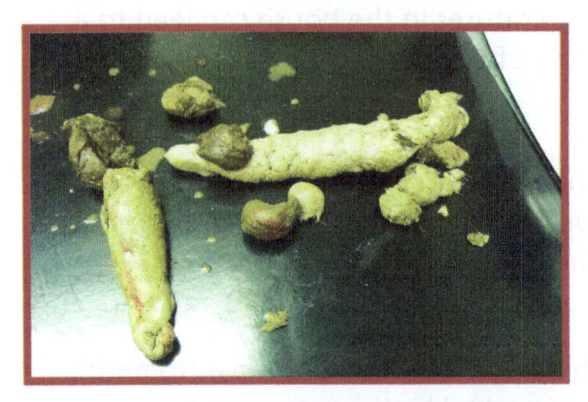

Constipation is when a snake cannot pass poo (faeces). If your snake is constipated you might notice him straining to pass faeces or that his faeces look very dry.

Faeces removed from one constipated snake

The temperature in your snake's house is vital. If it is too cold the intestines cannot digest food properly and this can lead to constipation.

Calcium is needed to make the intestines work properly. Ensure that your snake's UV light is at the correct height and is not too old.

It is very important that your snake has water at all times and that the humidity in his house is at the correct level. Dehydration often leads to constipation.

Be sure your snake is eating the correct type and amount of food. If he is greedy his intestines may become too full and therefore prone to impaction.

This condition is often left until it is too late. If an impaction is very severe an operation may be necessary to remove the material blocking the intestine.

PROLAPSE OF THE VENT

A prolapse happens when one of the organs plumbed into the vent, (for example the large intestine) gets pushed out of the body. Egg binding and a low calcium diet can cause a vent prolapse.

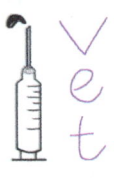

Vet — This is an emergency. If you suspect a prolapse you must take your snake to the vet as soon as possible.

CRYPTOSPORIDIUM

Cryptosporidium is an infection caused by a single celled organism called a protozoa. Infected snakes regurgitate their food and will lose weight. It is also very infectious.

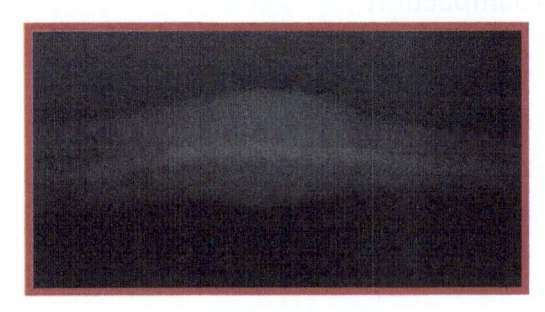

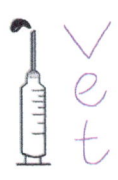

An x ray of swollen stomach

Vet — If your snake vomits or regurgitates he will need to see the vet. This condition is very difficult to treat.

32

LUNGS

Inside the bodies of mammals there is a big sheet of muscle, called the diaphragm. This separates the chest, where the lungs are, and the abdomen, where the stomach and intestines are. Your snake has no diaphragm. His chest and abdomen share the same space.

Partly because they have no diaphragm snakes are unable to cough. This can be a problem because if they get a build-up of fluid in their lungs, they are unable to clear it by coughing.

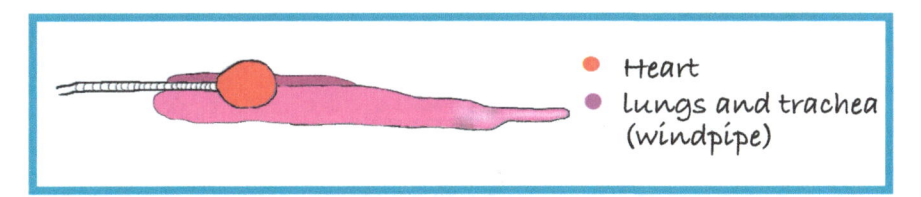

- Heart
- Lungs and trachea (windpipe)

LUNG PROBLEMS

PNEUMONIA- RESPIRATORY INFECTION

Pneumonia is an inflammation and infection of the lungs. It can be caused by viral and bacterial infection. There are two very important viruses that affect snakes.

These are called Ophidian Paramyxovirus and Inclusion Body Disease.

When you are going on holiday make sure that the snake is not left with or exposed to other snakes.

It is vital that the reptile house is kept at the correct temperature and has the correct level of humidity.

A good diet protects the immune system.

If your snake is showing signs of illness then you must take him to the vet.

HEART

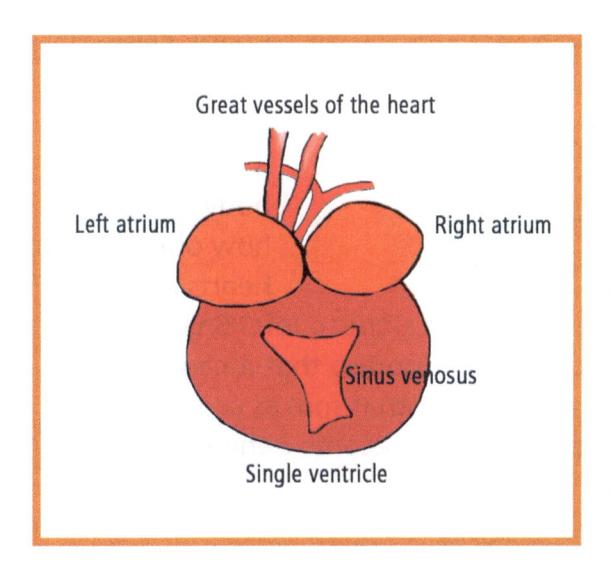

Great vessels of the heart
Left atrium
Right atrium
Sinus venosus
Single ventricle

The heart is a specialised muscle which collects blood full of oxygen from the lungs and pumps it around the body. It also collects blood full of carbon dioxide from the body and pumps it back to the lungs. This cycle goes on continuously.

The heart sits in the chest cavity in mammals and is divided into four chambers. The right atrium collects blood full of carbon dioxide from the body, sends it down to the right ventricle which then pumps it to the lungs. The left atrium collects blood full of oxygen from the lungs, sends it down to the left ventricle which pumps it around the body. Blood is constantly being pumped from right to left, via the lungs and travels around the body inside a series of tubes of varying diameters. These are known as blood vessels.

The heart of a snake differs from the heart of a mammal in several ways. It is especially adapted to suit the life of a reptile. The heart is roughly one third to one quarter down the length of the snake. Inside the heart of the snake there are three chambers; the right atrium, left atrium and the ventricle.

Great vessels leaving the heart

Left atrium   Right atrium

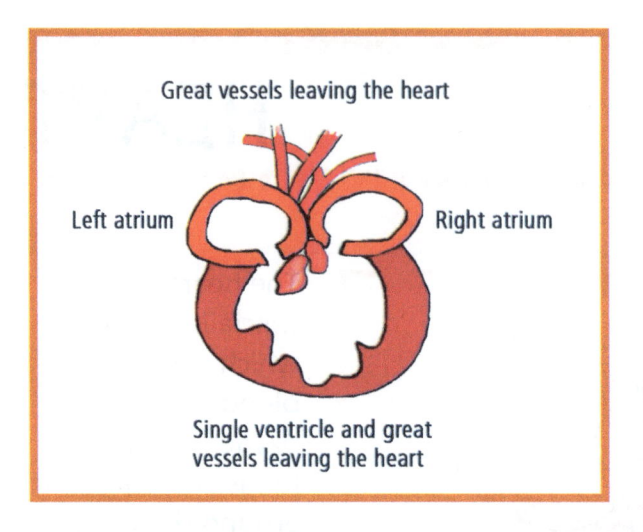

Single ventricle and great vessels leaving the heart

There is also an extra chamber outside the heart, called the sinus venosus which collects blood. Snakes can move blood to wherever it is needed in the body. Remember how our mammal hearts always pump blood round the body from right to left? Snakes can change the direction of the blood so that it can flow backwards. This is one of the ways that snakes can survive if they are short of oxygen or if they become dehydrated.

When a house is too cold, the heart cannot beat fast enough to keep the blood pumping to all the vital organs.

It is vital to provide a good source of UV light and a balanced diet. The heart is a muscle and needs a constant supply of calcium to enable it to beat properly.

36

HEART DISEASE

Heart disease is seen in snakes. It is most common in corn snakes. The heart is a muscle and it enlarges and does not pump properly. Snakes with heart disease are often quiet, do not move around and do not eat.

The snake on the right has an enlarged heart.

Any snake with heart disease will need treatment from the vet.

37

REPRODUCTIVE SYSTEM

The reproductive system is responsible for the production of sperm or eggs, mating, and the development of offspring. It varies depending on whether your snake is male or female. Even if your snake lives alone the reproductive system is still active and can develop problems.

Determining whether your snake is male or female is done by probing. This is where a small metal stick is inserted into the vent to find the hemipenes. In the male, the probe travels more than six scales and in the female less than six scales. Probing must to be done only by an experienced snake handler or vet.

MALES

Male snakes have two testicles which produce sperm. They are inside the body and near the kidneys. Instead of having one penis (willy) like mammals do, they have two. These are called hemipenes and are found inside the vent. Only one hemipene is used at a time for mating. The hemipenes do not carry urine the way that a mammals penis does.

HEMIPENE PROBLEMS

PROLAPSE

The hemipenes are normally inside the vent and only appear for mating. If a hemipene gets stuck outside the body this is known as a prolapse. A prolapsed hemipene can become damaged and infected.

If you think your snake has a prolapsed hemipene he needs to go to the vet. If the hemipene has suffered a lot of damage or has become infected he may need an operation to remove it.

ABSCESS

Sometimes a hemipene can become impacted with hard pus, forming an abscess. This is a common condition in male snakes.

It is important to keep his house at the correct temperature.

A good balanced diet will promote a healthy immune system, helping to fight infection.

If you suspect your snake has an abscessed hemipene you will need to take him to the vet. He may need an operation to remove the abscess or the hemipene.

Note that if a snake does need to have a hemipene removed he will still be able to breed, as he will be able to use his second hemipene.

FEMALES

Female snakes have two ovaries which produce eggs. They are found inside the body near the kidneys. They also have two oviducts. These are tubes along which the eggs are transported to the urodeum area of the vent. Snakes tend to lay large numbers of rubbery eggs. If they susccessfully mate with a male snake the eggs will hatch approximately 40-60 days later, depending on the species. However, female snakes can produce eggs without mating and sometimes this can lead to problems.

EGG PROBLEMS

FOLLICULAR STASIS AND EGG BINDING

Follicular stasis is a condition where the eggs do not develop properly and are without a shell. These undeveloped eggs remain inside the body and can make an affected snake very ill.

Egg binding is common in snakes. Here the eggs have been made and are fully developed but they become stuck inside the body and cannot be laid.

The house must be kept at the correct temperature. If it is too cold her body will struggle to make and lay eggs.

Dehydration will make it very difficult for your female snake to make and lay eggs.

Producing eggs uses a large amount of energy. Ensure that your snake has an adequate and balanced diet.

Your snake will need a hiding place in her house with plenty of substrate. This allows her to dig holes where she will bury her eggs.

If your snake develops any egg related problems she will need to visit the vet. Egg bound snakes need an operation to remove the retained eggs from the body. Follicular stasis can only be corrected by spaying. This is an operation to remove the ovaries and oviducts.

41

KIDNEYS

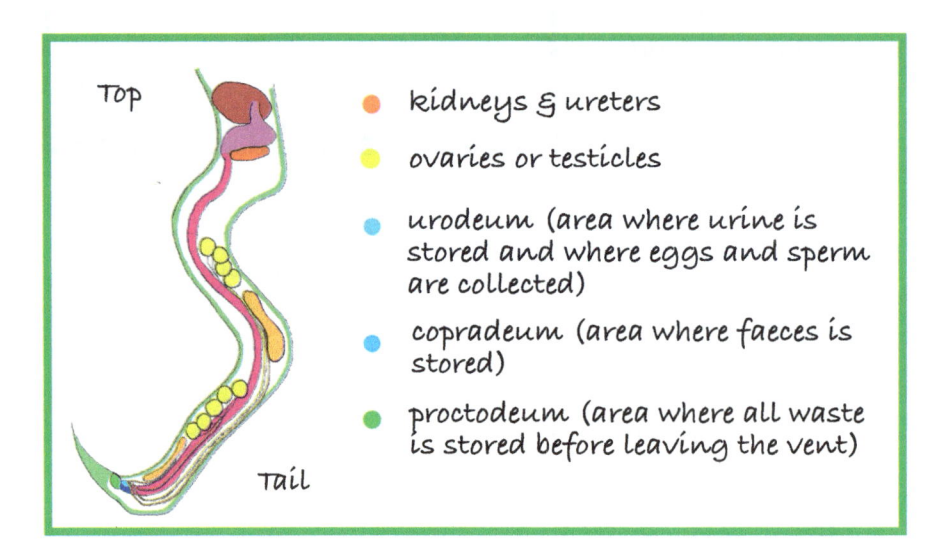

- kidneys & ureters
- ovaries or testicles
- urodeum (area where urine is stored and where eggs and sperm are collected)
- copradeum (area where faeces is stored)
- proctodeum (area where all waste is stored before leaving the vent)

Top / Tail

Mammals and snakes have two kidneys. The purpose of the kidneys is to remove poisonous waste material from the body.

THE MAMMAL KIDNEY

All fluid taken in by the body is processed by the kidneys. These include cups of tea, soft drinks and of course water. The kidney ensures that there is enough water to keep the body hydrated. Any water not required is stored in the bladder until it is passed as urine, which is a clear and yellow liquid.

THE REPTILE KIDNEY

The kidney of the reptile is different as it does not have the ability to retain water within the body. Reptile urine is a mixture of water and a solid white material called uric acid. The snake has developed unique ways to keep his body hydrated.

There is a small flap inside the urodeum that can move water into the large bowel where it is reabsorbed into the body. The snake can also suck water up through the vent whilst bathing. Their urine is stored in the urodeum and passes out of the body through the vent.

KIDNEY PROBLEMS

GOUT

Gout is a condition caused by too much uric acid in the body. The uric acid presents itself as solid white material which can easily be spotted in the urine. Sometimes these hard crystals deposit themselves in the muscles, joints and organs which can cause damage.

Make sure your snake always has enough water to drink. Dehydration can contribute to the development of gout.

Feed a balanced nutritious diet to your snake to prevent gout.

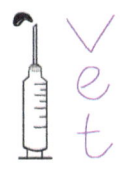

Gout is serious and will need veterinary treatment.

43

KIDNEY FAILURE

Many different diseases affect the kidneys. These include infections, inflammation and toxic damage. A snake with kidney failure will be less active than usual, lose his appetite, suffer weight loss and become dehydrated.

The house must be at the correct temperature.

Your snake needs to have access to drinking water.

Correct diet is important. Do not be tempted to feed cat food to your snake, as this could damage his kidneys. Do not over dust the insects with calcium powder as this can also damage the kidneys. A good diet also helps to support the immune system.

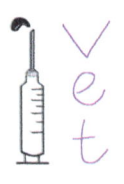

Any weight loss or change in eating habits needs a visit to the vet.

NUTRITIONAL DISEASE

Nutritional diseases are caused by feeding an incorrect diet. They can occur if fed too much or too little of the nutrients, vitamins and minerals needed to maintain good health. Nutritional disease is a common problem seen in snakes, yet it is preventable.

MALNUTRITION

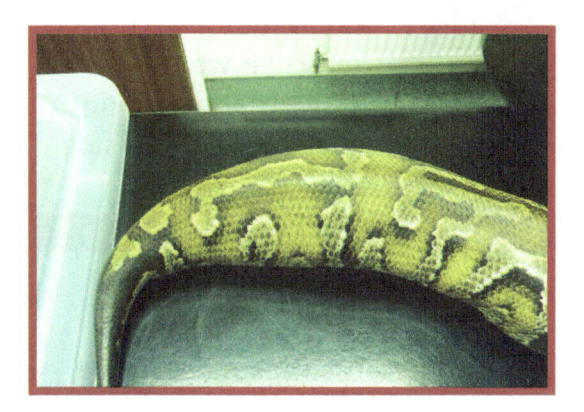

Malnutrition is a result of incorrect diet. This may be too much or too little of any food. The photograph shows a snake suffering from malnutrition. This snake is very fat.

Keeping your snake at the correct temperature helps his stomach and small intestine to absorb all the nutrients from his food.

Make sure you feed a varied diet to your snake.

45

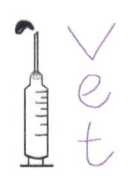

Vet Most cases of malnutrition need specialist veterinary care.

VITAMIN B DEFICIENCY

Snakes that eat fish can suffer from vitamin B1 deficiency. Freezing raw fish damages this vitamin.

Snakes with vitamin B1 deficiency show signs of muscular weakness and tremors and holding their head to one side.

VITAMIN D3 AND CALCIUM DEFICIENCY

Vitamin D3 and calcium are needed to keep your snake's bones strong and his muscles active. Deficiencies of these vitamins are not common. This is because snakes eat whole animals.

Keeping your snake at the correct temperature helps his stomach and small intestine to absorb all the nutrients from his food.

Make sure you feed a varied diet to your snake.

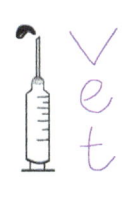

Vet If your snake has a nutritional disease he may have to visit the vet for vitamin injections and help with feeding.

ANOREXIA

Anorexia means that the snake is not eating. It is common for snakes not to eat in captivity. This can be very serious, especially if the snake does not eat for a long time. Some male snakes do not eat when they are near a female. Weight loss of more than 10% of the total body weight may harm the snake.

Make sure the house is at the correct temperature. Heat is needed to make the intestines work.

Dehydration can lead to anorexia.

Try to ensure that the food you feed is a close to the kind of food that the snake would eat in the wild. Many snakes will not eat unfamiliar food.

Vet Weight loss of more than 10% can be serious and may need a vet to check the snake and make sure there are no underlying diseases.

47

PARASITES

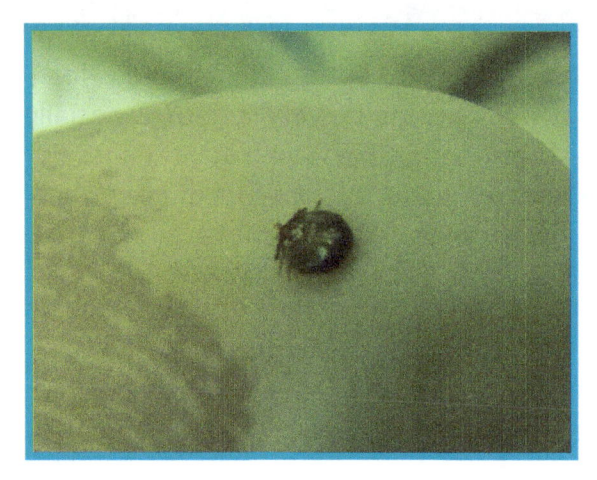

Parasites are creatures that feed off another animal. There are two basic types of parasites. Internal parasites live inside the body. External parasites live on the outside.

A tick

Roundworms and tapeworms are found inside the intestines. Mites and ticks are external parasites that suck the blood and bite the skin.

Snakes are also prone to infections by a single celled parasite called Cryptosporidium. It attacks the stomach lining and causes it to thicken. Snakes with this infection do not eat and usually vomit. This is a very infectious condition with no cure.

Vet: If you see any moving black or red dots on your snake's skin, or worms in his faeces, you need to take him to the vet. These are signs of parasites.

48

INFECTIOUS DISEASE

There are a number of viruses that can affect snakes. Fortunately these are not common. Ophidian Paramyxo Virus and Inclusion Body Disease cause anorexia, lung and brain infections. These viruses can be spread by mites.

Buying captive bred snakes and choosing holiday accommodation carefully reduces the risk of infection.

Bacteria and fungus can also be infectious.

Infections need treatment from a vet. Act quickly if you have a collection of reptiles to try and prevent spreading.

GROWTHS, TRAUMA & NEUROLOGICAL DISEASE

GROWTHS

This photograph shows a swelling on a corn snake.

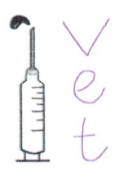

Vet

If you find any lump or swelling on your snake take him to the vet. To find out exactly what the growth is the vet may need to do some tests. It might be a tumour and some tumours are types of cancer that can then spread. However, the lumps may be abscesses or cysts. Some growths can be surgically removed.

TRAUMA

This snake got stuck in an ornamental skull that was in his house! He had to have an anaesthetic so the vet could cut the skull and release him.

If your snake has suffered any trauma or injury he must be taken to the vet to be checked and to receive any necessary treatment.

Neurological Disease

The brain and the spinal chord in snakes are similar to those found in mammals.

VITAMIN B DEFICIENCY

Some snakes eat fish. An example being the garter snake. In the wild this snake would catch and eat fresh fish. There are eight types of vitamin B. In snakes, vitamin B1 plays an important part in helping the brain to function correctly.

Captive snakes have to rely on a diet of fish that is often bought frozen and then thawed in small amounts ready for the snake's meal. The action of freezing damages vitamin B1. Over time this can lead to vitamin B1 deficiency. Therefore, extra vitamin B needs to be added to the prepared fish in the form of a vitamin powder.

Snakes with Vitamin B deficiency show signs of muscular weakness and tremors.

Ensure the house is warm to help with the digestion process of food.

A good balanced diet, with calcium and vitamin supplements is essential to ensure the muscles work correctly.

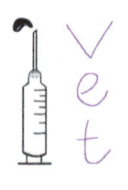

Vitamin B deficiency will need injections from the vet.

VIRAL DISEASE

There are two very important viruses that affect snakes. These are called Ophidian Paramyxovirus and Inclusion Body Disease. Both cause inflammation of the brain and are very serious infections.

These are highly infectious and need to be taken to the vets immediately.

SKELETON

Snakes have evolved so that they move very efficiently along the ground and up into trees without the use of legs. Most snakes have no legs at all. However, some snakes have vestigial (remnants) of back legs around the vent.

Movement is by contractions of muscles and rippling the body in an s shape. The body of the snake is protected by ribs and these are present all the way down to the level of the vent.

SPINAL OSTEOARTHROPATHY

This is a condition seen in snakes. The back bone becomes infected with bacteria. The body tries to fight the infection which then leads to the bones breaking and trying to fuse.

Vet

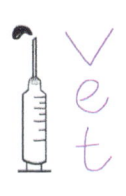

If you suspect your snake has this condition you must visit the vet as soon as possible.

INDEX

A

abdomen 33
abscesses 15
anus 26
atrium 35

B

blood vessels 35
brain 49, 51
burns 16

C

calcium 31
cancer 50
carbon dioxide 35
chambers 35
choana 26
constipation 30
coprodeum 28
cornea 22
cough 33
cryptosporidium 32, 48

D

diaphragm 33
digestive system 26
dysecdysis 14

E

egg binding 32, 40
eggs 27, 42
external parasites 48

F
faeces 27, 42
fatty liver disease 30
follicular stasis 40, 41

G
gout 43
growth 13, 50

H
heart V
hemipene 38, 39, 40
hepatic lipidosis 30

I
impaction 31
inclusion body disease 34
internal parasites 48
intestines 9, 26, 31, 33, 47, 48
iris 21

K
kidney failure 44
kidneys 42

L
liver 27
lump 50

M
mites 18, 25, 49
mouth 26, 27, 29
mouth rot 29

N
neurological disease VII, 51, 53
nutritional disease 45

O
oesophagus 27
ophidian paramyxo virus 49
ovaries 42
oxygen 35, 36

P
pancreas 27
parasites 48
penis 38
pneumonia 33
proctodeum 27, 42
prolapse 32, 38

R
reproductive system 38
roundworms 48

S
scleral ossicles 22
shedding (ecdysis) 14
sinus venosus 36
skin 10, 13, 14, 15, 16, 17, 18, 19, 20, 21, 23, 48
spectacle 13, 19, 23, 25
sperm 27, 42
spinal chord 51
spinal osteoarthropathy 53
stomach 27
stomatitis 29

T
tapeworms 48
testicles 42
ticks 48
trauma 22, 23, 51
tumour 50

U
ulcer 22
uric acid 42, 43
urine 27, 42
urodeum 27, 42

V
vent 27, 42
ventricle 35, 36
vitamin a 46, 47
vitamin d3 10, 13

W
willy 38